HOW TO GET A
SHAG
IN 59 LANGUAGES

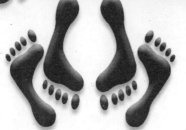

Crombie Jardine
PUBLISHING LIMITED

13 Nonsuch Walk, Cheam, Surrey, SM2 7LG
www.crombiejardine.com

Published by Crombie Jardine Publishing Limited
First edition, 2006

ISBN 1-905102-40-2

Compiled and written by Charlotte Hathaway

Designed by www.glensaville.com
Printed & bound in the United Kingdom by
William Clowes Ltd, Beccles, Suffolk

Contents

H

I

J

K

R

S

T

U

W

Y

Introduction

Picture this scenario: you're in a bar, and you see the most beautiful, shag-able, creature standing not a short distance away. You know what you want that night, and you know that by rights it should end with an interlocking of thighs in a location of minimal importance and comfort. But there's a hitch: nobody seems to speak English anymore! It's like it's gone out of fashion or something. Now they have something called the International Language of Love, and you've no idea how that goes. What's more, last orders has been called and you're painfully aware that you don't have time to waste messing about with casual conversation to get some casual sex. You need a phrase and you need it now. I've solved your problem for you and travelled the globe (earning many a raised eyebrow and a slap in the face) collecting the very phrases you *need* to get you laid worldwide. So read on and become a cunning linguist!

A note to the reader

This book aims to provide the humble horny traveller with the much-desired translation of 'fancy a shag?', as well as predicted responses (be they a simple slap in the face, a cutting line, or glad acceptance).

HOWEVER, it is well to bear in mind that in many cultures even dropping hints in this direction may be considered deeply offensive, and although I have gathered the corresponding phrases to 'fancy a shag?', please don't write letters of complaint to my publisher when you find yourself locked in some obscure prison in some far distant land.

On pronunciation: I have done my best to transcribe pronunciation as accurately as possible without resorting to complex IPA (international phonetic alphabet), however I have given in to temptation and used a couple of symbols. These are:

ə = schwa – sounding sort of like 'uh', it is a neutral vowel that in English replaces any vowel in an unstressed syllable, for example the second 'a' in 'alphabet'.

ᵘs = glottal stop – this is the sound made when you are too lazy to say a letter, like the 't' in 'butter', making the word sound like 'bu'er'. The sound is made at the back of your throat and is like a stopping of breath before continuing with the word. If it comes at the end of a word, it may just sound like an abrupt stop.

All other words are written according to the spelling/pronunciation rules that would apply to a native English-speaker. It helps to try and say the phrases with the appropriate foreign accent (e.g. French sleaze or Swedish sing-song).

Good luck!

Charlotte Hathaway, 2006
comments to: charlotte@crombiejardine.com.

Afrikaans

Afrikaans is spoken in South Africa and Namibia, and is very closely related to Dutch. In fact the name means 'African' and is often seen as the African form of Dutch. South Africa has had a turbulent history, however now it prides itself in being better than us at the sports we invented.

Fancy a shag?

Wil jy naai?

(Fancy a shag?)
pronounced: Wil yai nay?

Wil jy seks hê?

(Would you like to have sex? – quite formal)
pronounced: Wil yai sex hay?

You're on!

O ja!

(Yes please!)
pronounced: U yah!

The brush—off

Nee!

(No!)
pronounced: Nia!

Classical Arabic

Colloquial Arabic is different in each country where it is spoken, however Classical Arabic is universal throughout the Arab world. As Classical Arabic is a holy language and is used primarily for religious and formal occasions, use it wisely so as to cause as little offence as possible. Here are some useful phrases, as well as the expected responses:

Fancy a shag?

ابنتك بمئة جمل

(100 camels for your daughter)
pronounced: Ibnatuka bi mi'ati jamal

أتريدين ممارسة الجنس؟

(Would you like to practise sex?)
pronounced: Atoreedeen
mumarasat el jinsi?

You're on!

حسنا

(OK)
pronounced: Hasanan (the 'H' is very hard, like
you're choking, or with 'closed throat')

نعم

(Yes)
pronounced: Na'am

يجوز

(Possible)
pronounced: Yajooz ('j' here is like
the middle of 'measure')

جائز
(Permitted)
pronounced: Ja^usiz

The brush-off

لا

(No)
pronounced: La

شكرا

(No ('thanks' and shake your head))
Pronounced: Shukran
N.B. Owing to the pedantry of grammar, the
questions can only be asked by a man.

Jordanian Arabic

This is a colloquial form of Arabic spoken in Jordan in non-formal situations. While getting laid by Jordan may be every young man's dream, getting laid in Jordan may be the next best thing... Try some of these phrases and remember that Jordan has much more to offer than just Page 3 tits.

Fancy a shag?

تنتاكي

(Do you want to be fucked? –
only works for addressing girls)
pronounced: Tintaki?

توكليه؟

(Do you want to eat it? – to female)
pronounced: Tuklee?

توكله؟

(Do you want to eat it? – to male)
pronounced: Toklo?

You're on!

ليش لأ

(Why not?)
pronounced: Leesh la?

ماشي

(Ok)
pronounced: Maashi

The brush-off

أختك ابتنتاك؟

(Would your sister want to be fucked?)
pronounced: Ukhtak ibtintak ('kh' is a bit similar
to Scottish 'ch' but a bit harder)

أختك ابتوكله؟

(Does your sister eat it?)
pronounced: Ukhtak ibtoklo?

يا وقح

(You rude person)
pronounced: Ya wi'iih

هلأ بصيح وبلم الحارة عليك

(If you don't go away I will scream and get the
neighbourhood onto you – to male)
pronounced: Halla' baseeH wi ballem il Hara
aleek (the 'H' is very hard, like you're choking, or
with 'closed throat')

حل عني

(Get away from me)
pronounced: Hill anni

Basque

Basque is spoken in the Pyrénées, more specifically the Basque Country, which is made up of the Spanish provinces of Álava, Vizcaya, and Guipúzcoa. As a language, Basque is not related to any of the other Indo-European languages. In a country whose name is synonymous with erotic lingerie, you can't lose!

Fancy a shag?

Larrua joko gogorik baduzu?

(Do you fancy getting laid?)
pronounced: Lah-roo-ah ho-koh
go-go-rick bah-doo-soo?

You're on!

Gustura! Nire jaka ekarri behar naiz!

(With pleasure! I am going to get my coat!)
pronounced: Ch-oo-stoo-rah! Nee-reh
cha-kah eh-car-ree beh-are nigh-ees!

The brush-off

Zu itusia zara eta dena den, ez zara atsegin zaidan horietakoa

(You're ugly and anyway you're not my type)
pronounced: Sue ee-too-see-ah sah-rah eh-tah den-ah den, ess sah-rah at-say-ch-een sigh-dan or-yet-ah-ko-ah
N.B. 'ch' as in 'loch'

Bosnian

Bosnia, made famous by its wars, is part of the state of Bosnia and Herzogovina, renowned for its various Eurovision entries. Map-makers (or cartographers as they like to call themselves) believe that it can be found in South East Europe. Bosnian is a Slavic language, and uses both Cyrillic and Latin script, as well as a few other scripts native to Bosnia.

Fancy a shag?

`oćeš malo hopa–cupa?

(Fancy a shag?)
pronounced: 'Ochesh malo hopa–tsoopa?

You're on!

Vala, ajde. Naćemo se napolju za deset minuta

(Yes please, meet you outside in 10 minutes)
pronounced: Valla, aydə. Nachemo se napol–yoo za deset minoota

The brush-off

Goni se, seljaćino

(Get lost, you pervert)
pronounced: Goni se, sel-yacheeno

Breton

Breton is a Celtic language of the Brythonic (or P-Celtic) variety (sort of like Welsh and Cornish) and is spoken in Brittany in France. However, unfortunately for Breton speakers, the French state does not recognise it as an official language. This particular dialect is the Trégor dialect, spoken in North West Côtes d'Armor and North East Finistère. Asterix look-a-likes will be your main targets here, and if that's your type...

Fancy a shag?

Deus da c'hwari koukoug ganin!

(Come play cuckoo with me!)
pronounced: Ders də hwa–ee koo–kook gəneen!

You're on!

A ya, ma kerez!

(Oh yes, if you like!)
pronounced: A yah, mə kayrəs!

Gwres ma jeu din, paotr koant/plac'h koant!

(Give me the works – lit. 'do my stuff to me'
– pretty boy/pretty girl!)
pronounced: Gwrayz mə zyoer deen, poat kwann

/plach kwann! (zy is like the 's' in 'vision', 'ch' as in Scottish 'loch')

The brush-off

A nann! Kês da stoupad, kozh porc'hell hudur!

(Oh no! Buzz off, you disgusting old pig!)
pronounced: A nann! Case də stoopət, koois puhr-həl hooi-dooir!

Gant ur strouilhenn ssort dit-te, biken!

(With a slagger the likes of you, never!)
pronounced: Gann err strooyən sərd deetay, beekən!

Cantonese

'Cantonese' is used to refer to one of the three main spoken dialects of Chinese (a written language). Cantonese and Mandarin are pronounced differently, but written almost indentically. Of the two, Cantonese is probably the more common outside of China – and Cantonese people can be found in every tourist location, university, and private school in Britain. Mind you check whether your victim speaks Cantonese or Mandarin before leaping into action.

Fancy a shag?

可唔可以同我上床呀?

(Fancy a shag?)

pronounced: Hor mm hor e tonn or shan chon ar?

You're on!

好呀, 10 分鐘之後係 出面見啦

(Yes please, meet you outside in 10 minutes)

pronounced: Ho ar, sub fun jong dzi how high chur mean ggin la.

The brush-off

唔好掂我,走開呀變態佬!

(No, go away you pervert!)

pronounced: Mm ho dim or, zou hoi ar bin thai lo!

Catalan

Catalan is the national language of Andorra, and is also spoken in several areas of Spain, being that country's second most widely spoken language. Speakers of Catalan can also be found in parts of France and Italy. Andorra's tiny size leads to obvious questions about inbreeding. Your advances have a high chance of success therefore, as your target will be so relieved that you're not a blood relative they'll probably say yes to anything.

Fancy a shag?

Vols follar?

(Fancy a shag?)
pronounced: Bols fuhya?

You're on!

Sí, esclar, m'agradaria molt!

(Yes please, I'd love it!)
pronounced: See, əskla, məghrudaria mol!

The brush-off

Vés a la merda!

(Fuck off! – lit. 'go to the shit')
pronounced: Bays ə lə mairdə!

Chichewa

Chichewa is one of the two official national languages of Malawi, in South East Africa, along with English. It is also spoken in Mozambique, Zambia, and Zimbabwe. Due to issues of AIDS, we would recommend the use of a condom at all costs when you meet with success after using these sure-fire lines.

Fancy a shag?

Muruwa kugowa pamodi/pamodzi?

(Fancy a shag? – male version/female version)
pronounced: as written

You're on!

Ndi funa!

(Yes!)
pronounced: as written

Inde!

(I want!)
pronounced: as written

The brush-off

Choka/chokani!

(Bugger off! – male version/female version)
pronounced: as written

Croatian

This is a Slavic language which is 100% mutually intelligible with Bosnian and Serbian. And, funnily enough, it is spoken in Croatia, Bosnia and Herzegovina, and Serbia and Montenegro. Croatia is known for its lovely beaches and new floods of British tourists. Try to avoid these (the tourists, I mean, not the beaches).

Fancy a shag?

Jesi li za ševu?

(Fancy a shag?)
pronounced: Yeysee lee za shevoo?

You're on!

Što da ne? Vidimo se vani za deset minuta
(Why not? See you outside in 10 minutes)
pronounced: Shto da ney?
Videemo se vanee za deset minoota

The brush-off

Ne, skote jedan perverzni

(No, piss off you pervert)
pronounced: Ney, skotə yeydan perverznee

Czech

Czech is a Slavic language which closely resembles Slovak and Polish, and is spoken in the Czech Republic, Germany and Slovakia. The Czech Republic's capital, Prague, is one of Europe's newest, most fashionable tourist destinations, popular with budget airlines. If you do find a solitary Czech person amongst the droves of tourists, these phrases may come in handy:

Fancy a shag?

Seš kus, nezašukáme si?

(You're a piece, shan't we shag?)
pronounced: Sash koos, neyzashucamma see?

You're on!

Jasně, brouku, ale v autě to moc nemusím

(Sure bug, but in the car I don't really have to
(= I don't really want to in the car)).
Pronounced: Yas-nhe broke-oo, ahlley v*
aw-che toe moss ney-moo-seam
(*like the first 'v' in vent without
the 'e' sound after)

The brush-off

Co kdyby sis místo toho obtěžování a ztrapňování se strčil ptáka do vysavače

(How about instead of bothering me and embarrassing yourself you go stick your bird (=penis) in a vacuum?)

pronounced: So kdeebie sees me-stow toe-ho obchejou-vah-nhee ah strapnho-vah-nhee say stir-chill ptah-kah do* vee-sah-vah-che?
(*like 'doe' but with a short 'o')

N.B. In the Czech Republic a woman probably wouldn't ask a man for sex, so the last response only works one-way. Anyway, what man would ever refuse an offer of sex from a woman?

Danish

A Scandinavian language spoken in
Denmark, Germany (Schleswig-Holstein),
the Faroe Islands, and Greenland. The
Danes have a history of invading and
owning other countries (perhaps due to
an inferiority complex about not quite
living up to the Swedes' reputation of
acknowledged sex-appeal). However,
the Danes *are* attractive, and should
you ever find yourself in their incredibly
expensive country, these phrases
might help. Remember you want to
pull a great Dane, but not a dog!

Fancy a shag?

Lyst til at bolle?

(Fancy a shag?)
pronounced: Luust (really deep 'u' sound
with lips pursed) til at bo-lə?

Med på at bolle?

(Fancy a shag?)
pronounced: Me' po at bo-lə?

You're on!

Yep – meget gerne!

(Yes I'd love to!)
pronounced: Yep– mah–ll (really open mouth
with the 'a') ger–nə!

The brush–off

Skrid!

(Piss off!)
pronounced: Skri'!
(the final 'd' isn't really pronounced and you
get a kind of 'l' sound. Also, the 'r' has to be
pronounced as in German, with the throat
and not at the front of the mouth)

Doric

Doric is a dialect of Lowland Scots, spoken in North East Scotland. Its name comes from references to Dorian Greeks, who lived in Sparta. Lowland Scots is used extensively in literature (see Sir Walter Scott or Robert Burns), and is a Germanic language often thought to be a debased form of English. It is now fighting for its right to legitimate minority language status in Scotland. If you've ever complained about not being able to understand a Scotsman, don't worry; he may not even have been speaking English. This particular form of Doric is specific to Forfar, Angus.

Fancy a shag?

Hi, quine! Fid ye fancy hain a wee drammle o hochmagandy ahint the haywain?

(I say, young lady! Would you like to have carnal relations behind that hay bale?)
pronounced: as written, with Scots accent

Fid ye like me tae loup yer banes?

(Would you like me to jump your bones?)
pronounced: as written, with Scots accent

You're on!

Aye! Meet me ahint the kine shed in half an 'oor!

(Yes! Meet me behind the cow
shed in half an hour!)
pronounced: as written, with Scots accent

Aye, that'd be gae braw! Ye can faur far whaur than haen a wee trammel hochmagandy erst hing o a morning

(Yes, that sounds dandy! You can do
much worse than having a little bit of sex
first thing in the morning)
pronounced: as written, with Scots accent

The brush-off

Nut, yer bowfin'

(No, you're distinctly unpleasant)
pronounced: as written, with Scots accent

Och, I divnae ken aboot that. But al gie ye a wee bosey instid

(Oh, I don't know about that. But I'll give you a little hug/snuggle instead)
pronounced: as written, with Scots accent

Awa! Ging fuck yersel ye clorty sasannach/teuchter!

(Away! Go fuck yourself you filthy sasannach
(derogatory term for an English person)/teuchter
(derogatory term for a country person))
pronounced: as written, with Scots accent
(note 'ch' is soft as in 'loch')

Dutch

This is a West Germanic language similar to German, and is spoken mostly in the Netherlands and Belgium, and also in Suriname, Aruba, the Netherlands Antilles, Indonesia, and some parts of France. The Dutch are a liberal people with liberal laws, however in certain parts of Amsterdam you will have to negotiate a price rather than use chat-up lines.

Fancy a shag?

Heb je zin om te neuken?

(Fancy a shag?)
pronounced: Hep yeh zeen om tə noegen?

Heb je zin om te palen?

(Fancy a shag? – more colloquial, palen is a more
degenerative word for sex)
pronounced: Hep yeh zeen om tə pahleh?
(the 'p' in 'palen' is closer to 'b')

You're on!

Ja natuurlijk jij geil beest

(Yes, of course, you horny beast)
pronounced: Yə natooleg ye cheəl baste
(the 'ch' is like in Scottish 'loch',
but with more phlegm)

The brush-off

Nee, flikker op viezerik

(No, sod off you pervert)
pronounced: Nay, flicker opp fee-zyureek
(that last bit is said like 'Zurich', but with
emphasis on the last syllable)

Elvish (Quenya)

'What's going on? This isn't a real language!'
I hear you cry. Well, the great man Tolkien
did create a very complex and structured
language, and many people out there in the
world claim to be able to speak it. These
phrases could come in very handy if you
happen to stumble across a beautiful geek
you wish to impress. Quenya is High Elven,
one of the two most complete of Tolkien's
Elven languages. I also include some
repostes in what is known as 'fan-Elvish'
(used in role-playing games etc), which has
more scope for diverse phrases, and one
that said geek may be more familiar with
(depending on his/her level of geekiness).

The Tengwar Annatar type family font as used here, on pages 56-59, is the
property of the creator, Johan Winge, copyright © 2004-2006.

Fancy a shag?

﬩ﱞﱞﱞ ﱞﱞﱞ ﱞﱞﱞﱞﱞ

(You want to lie down with me?)
pronounced: Merit caita asinye?
(the 'ai' of 'caita' is pronounced as in 'aisle' –
not as in 'mail' – and 'asinye' is accented
on the middle syllable)

﬩ﱞﱞﱞ ﱞﱞﱞﱞ

(You want sex?)
pronounced: Merit puhta?
(the 'h' of 'puhta' is like the 'ch' of
Scottish 'loch'. The 'u' in this word is
pronounced as in 'put', not as in 'but')

ᚱᚱᚢ ᚢᚦ ᚾ ᚦᛟᛁ: ᛁ ᚦᛁᛁᚦᛏ ᛁᛁᚾ ᛁ
ᚱᚱᚦᛈᛈᚾ ᛈᛁᛁᚱ:

(Your hair shines like gold. Come outside with me
and look at the constellations)
pronounced: Findelya cala ve laure. A hótule
asinye i meneltannar tirien ('ó' as in 'cold')

ᛁ ᚷᚦᛈ ᛁᚾ ᛈᚦᛈ ᛈᚦᚱᚱᚱ

(Take off your clothes and lie down on the bed!)
pronounced: A helta ar caita caimanna!

You're on!

ᚱᚱᚱ ᚱᛁᚱᛈᚱ

(Your place or mine?)
pronounced: Mano mardenna?

ᴹᴱᴸᴸᴲ ᴶᴦ ᴾ� ᴳ ᴹᴺ ᴼᴾᴮ

(Your beauty shines bright, shall we go?)
(fan Elvish)
pronounced: Vanimle sila tiri lle merna aut?
('au' like 'ou' in 'house')

The brush-off

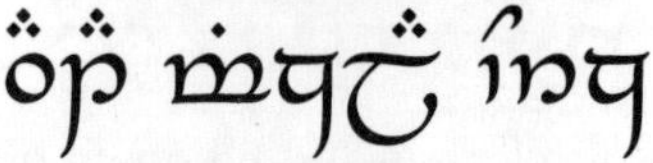

ᴼᴾ ᴹᴪ ᴶᴴ

(Go kiss an orc)
(fan Elvish)
pronounced: Auta miqula orqu

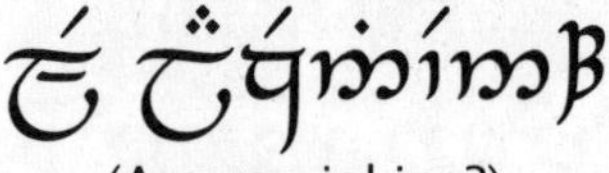

ᴳ ᴛᴴᴹᴵᴹᴮ

(Are you joking?)
(fan Elvish)
pronounced: Lle lakwenien?

ᚹᚾ ᛗᛟᛗᛗᛏ ᛁᚾ ᚢ ᛁᛈᚤ ᛏᛗᛁᛏᛏ

(You're ugly and your mother dresses you funny)
(fan Elvish)
pronounced: Llie n'vanima ar' lle atara lanneina
('ei' as in 'eight')

Estonian

Estonian is related to Finnish and Hungarian, and is spoken in Estonia (no surprises there). Estonia is another country thrown into the Western European eye by its various (and sometimes successful) Eurovision entries. I believe it lies in northern Europe, near Finland, Sweden and Russia, and increasing numbers of British tourists are proving that its location and existence are more than just cartographic conspiracy.

Fancy a shag?

Teeme ühe kähkuka?

(Fancy a shag?)
pronounced: Teemə uhə kahkooka?
(N.B. 'ü' = u in surreal, 'ä' = a in cat,
'õ' = o in slogan)

Kas sa magaksid minuga?

(Will you sleep with me?)
pronounced: Kas sa magaksid minooga?

You're on!

Tore, kohtume väljas kümne minuti pärast

(Please, meet you outside in 10 minutes)
pronounced: Torə, kohtoomə valyas kumnə minooti parast

The brush-off

Ei, tõmba uttu pervert

(No, sod off you pervert)
pronounced: Ei, toemba oottoo pervert

Faroese

Faroese is spoken in the Faroes, a small group of islands which lie between Shetland and Iceland. It is also spoken in parts of Denmark and Iceland. It is very close to Old Norse, Norn (now an extinct language but which was once spoken in Shetland, Orkney and Caithness), and Icelandic, with some Celtic influences. The name 'Faroe Islands' means 'sheep islands' and, well, the Faroese men like their sheep almost as much as they like their women. They also like to eat pilot whale, served with something that looks and tastes suspiciously like strawberry jam.

Fancy a shag?

Kom og mogga!

(Come and shag!
– 'At mogga' is an old word, which
means 'to cut with a blunt knife')
pronounced: Kom o' mogga!

You're on!

OK, (heima) hjá mær ella hjá tær?

(OK, your place or mine?)
pronounced: OK, (hima – 'i' as in 'bite') cha mair
edla cha tair ('r' is pronounced)?

The brush-off

Nei, takk, tú ert ikki mín typa

(No thanks, you're not my type)
pronounced: Noi, tahk, too ert (short 'e' as in 'bet', and 'r' pronounced) ich-i moin tupa

Filipino

Filipino, along with English, is the national language of the Philippines. It is based on Tagalog, which is also spoken in the Philippines. In fact many people claim that Filipino is Tagalog, just with a different name. If you look hard enough, you can locate the Philippines in South East Asia in the Malay Archipelago; it is made up of 7,107 islands.

Fancy a shag?

Gusto mo nang cantot?

(Fancy a shag?)
pronounced: as written

You're on!

O sige, bahay mo o bahay ko?

(Yeah ok, your place or mine?)
pronounced: as written

The brush-off

Ako'y bakla

(I'm gay)
pronounced: as written

Hindi, alis ka sa akin

(No, get away from me)
pronounced: as written

Suomi Finnish

Finnish is spoken in Finland and parts of northern Sweden, and is related to Hungarian. It has a reputation for being extremely difficult to understand and learn, so it is with great triumph that I bring you these few humble sentences, gained at great personal cost. Though Finland counts as part of Scandinavia, its language is completely unrelated to the rest of the Scandinavian languages. Looking good is a must on any night out on the pull in Finland, but watch out those Lapland winters don't catch you out if you think of using the age-old tactic of 'undress to impress'.

Fancy a shag?

Annaks mulle?

(Fancy a shag?)
pronounced: Annaks mulleh?
('e' is pronounced as in 'bet', 'l's are
not soft, like in eel or ill)

You're on!

Ok, meillä vai teillä?

(Ok, your place or mine?)
pronounced: Ok ('o' like in 'on') meilla vai teilla?
('ä' as in 'cat', the 't' is not aspirated, meaning
there is no small puff of air immediately after it
like in 'train' or most English words)

The brush-off

Ei kiitos, en antas sulle vaikka olisit viimene ihminen maailmassa!

(No thanks, I wouldn't shag you if you were the last person on Earth!)
pronounced: Ei keetos, en antas sulleh
('u' as in 'put') vaika olisit veemeneh
ihminen ma-ailmassa!

Flemish

Not 'similar to something you might cough up when you have a cold', but a real live language spoken in Belgium. Like many nations these days, Belgium is selfish and requires more than one national language, the other being French. Flemish is a form of Dutch spoken in Flanders, in the North of Belgium. Belgium is famous for its chocolate and its hosting of major international organisations. Are these two factors linked? I believe a detailed Government-funded study would give us the answer.

Fancy a shag?

Zin in een wip?

(Fancy a shag?)
pronounced: Zinn in eyn wip?

You're on!

Ja, dat zie ik wel zitten. Bij jou of bij mij thuis?

(Yes, that sounds great! Your place or mine?)
pronounced: Yah, dat zee ik well zitten.
Bay yau off bay may toes?
('oe' sound is something between 'oe'
and 'u' as in dust, but longer)

The brush-off

Neen, je bent mijn type niet

(No, you're not my type)
pronounced: Nehn, yeh bent mayn tippə neet

Neen, niet geïnteresseerd, zelfs niet al was je de laatste persoon op aarde

(No, not interested, and wouldn't be if you were the last person on Earth)
pronounced: Nehn, neet che-interressehrt ('ch' as in 'loch'), zelfs neet al was (rhymes with 'gas') yeh the latstə (long 'a') persohn op ahrdə ('r' rolled)

French

The French really require, and deserve, no introduction. However, due to my extreme generosity, I shall explain that they live across the English Channel, have invaded the English many times, and speak this so-called 'Romance language'. Whilst you do your quick duty-free shop in Calais, it may be as well to keep these phrases handy:

Fancy a shag?

Tu veux baiser?

(Fancy a shag?)
pronounced: Too və beysay?

Laisse-moi te prendre ma chérie!

(Let me take you darling!)
pronounced: Less mwa tə prondr ma sherry!

C'est le coup de foudre bébé!

(It's love at first sight, baby!)
pronounced: Sayh lə coop də foodr behbeh!

You're on!

Mais oui, tu es bien monté(e)!

(But yes, you are well endowed!)
pronounced: May wee, too ey bee–a(n) mo(n)tay!
(go as if to pronounce the 'n', then stop just
before you do)

On va chez moi ou chez toi?

(Your place or mine?)
pronounced: O(n) va shay mwa oo shay twa?

The brush-off

Vas te faire foutre

(Go fuck yourself)
pronounced: Va tə fair footr

Combien de gosses as-tu?

(How many kids do you have?)
pronounced: Combee-a(n) də goss a-too?

Tu es un homme/une femme refoulé(e) et depravé(e)!

(You are a repressed and depraved man/woman!)
pronounced: Too ey uhn-om/oon
fam rəfoolay ey deprahvay!

Scots Gaelic

An official minority language in Scotland,
it is spoken in the Highlands, Western
Isles, parts of Glasgow, and in Canada (in
Cape Breton, Nova Scotia). Gaelic has close
links with Irish and Manx, the Q-Celtic
branch of the Celtic family. Should you
ever find yourself lost and lonely in Lewis,
these phrases should do the trick. And if
the reply isn't 'baaaaa', then here are also
some phrases to help you understand
the response...

Fancy a shag?

Am bheil thu pòsda?

(Are you married? – very important
that this is established first)
pronounced: A vel oo posta?
(as in 'foster' but with a long 'o')

As 'fheàrr leat caileagan, balaich, no caoraich?

(Do you prefer girls, boys, or sheep?)
pronounced: A-shar lat call–yagan,
balich, no cerich?
(the 'o' in 'no' is as in 'pot', the 'er'
in 'cerich' is as in 'pervert')

Eil thu ag iarraidh bìdeag?

(Fancy a shag?)
pronounced: Ell oo ak–eeary beedjag?

You're on!

Tha gu dearbh!

(Yes please!)
pronounced: Haa goo djeh-rav!

The brush-off

'S fhada chitheann thu!

(Not as long as I can see you!)
pronounced: Sada chee-hen oo!

Thalas cac àrd a'bhacan

(I'll shit on you from a height)
pronounced: Halas cak ard a-vakan

Pòg mo thòn

(Kiss my ass)
pronounced: Pog mo hon (the 'o' is long,
except in 'mo', where it is as in 'not')
N.B. 'ch' is as in Scottish 'loch'

German

German is spoken in Germany, Switzerland, Austria, Belgium, Lichtenstein, and various other countries, though dialects and accents differ in different areas. The Germans take swearing a lot more lightly than most (and in a language where every word sounds like a curse, this is easy to do), so these phrases are cruder than some of the examples I have given you so far.

Fancy a shag?

Willst Du mit mir schlafen?

(Will you sleep with me?)
pronounced: Vilst doo mit mere shlaughen?
(like 'laugh', with 'sh' and 'en' added)

Lust auf 'ne Nummer/ 'nen Quicky?

(Fancy a shag?)
pronounced: Lust owf 'nə numer/
'nən quickie? ('u' as in 'put')

Willst Du ficken/poppen/ bumsen/rammeln?

(Fancy a shag? – more crude)
pronounced: Vilst doo fikken/poppen/bumsen/
rameln? ('u' in 'bumsen' as in 'put')

Wie wär's mit 'nem Dreier?

(Fancy a threesome?)
pronounced: Vee vear's mit 'nəm dryer?
('vear' like 'wear')

You're on!

Ja, sehr gerne.
Nimm mich jetzt!

(Yes I'd love to. Take me now!)
pronounced: Yah, sehr gehrnə. Nim mich yetz!

Lass es uns auf dem Rücksitz deines Autos treiben!

(Let's do it in the back seat of your car!)
pronounced: Lass ess uns owf dem rook-sitz
dye-nəs owtos try-ben! ('u' in 'uns' as in 'put')

Fick mich bis zum Morgengrauen!

(Fuck me till dawn!)
pronounced: Fikk mich biss zum morgengr-ow-en!
('u' as in 'put', 'grau' rhymes with 'plough', not 'grow')

The brush-off

Scheiße, nein. Verpiß Dich/ hau ab/Zieh' Leine!

(Shit, no. Piss off!)
pronounced: Sh-eye-sə, nine. Ferpiss dich/how ap/zee line-ə!

Nimm deine dreckigen Finger von mir, Drecksack!

(Take your fucking fingers off me, jerk!)
pronounced: Nim dye-nə dreckigen
fing-er fon mere, dreck-zack!

Steck dir doch 'ne Gurke 'rein, du hässliche Drecksschlampe!

(Plug a cucumber instead, you ugly slut!)
pronounced: Shteck dear doch nə gurkə rine, doo
hesslichə drecks-shlampə!
(N.B. 'ch' is pronounced as in Scottish
'loch', not 'church')

Swiss German

Swiss German has been described as sounding like someone speaking German with a hot potato in their mouth, or speaking German with a Swedish accent. Swiss German and German German are entirely different dialects, and while your best Berlin accent may be good enough to woo in the Fatherland, try a little more Swiss before you let the cuckoo out of the clock (speaking whilst eating a hot potato at reader's own risk). The Swiss are known for their holey cheese, banks, pristine time-keeping, and obsessive neutrality.

Fancy a shag?

Chunsch go bumse?

(Do you come and shag?)
pronounced: Chunsh go bumsə?
('ch' like Scottish 'loch', but with more phlegm)

You're on!

Ok, i genau zwei Minute und zwänzg Sekunde!

(Ok, in exactly two minutes and twenty seconds!)
pronounced: Ok, ee gənow tsvai
minootə unt tsventsg zekundə!
('u' like in 'put', but long)

The brush-off

Piss di!

(Piss off!)
pronounced: Piss dee!

Greek

Greek is spoken in Greece and in Cyprus. Greece is home to the people who brought you philosophy, feta cheese, and Faliraki, as well as a whole load of exciting mythology popular with primary school teachers and Classics professors.

Fancy a shag?

θέλεις γαμήσι;

(Fancy a shag?)
pronounced: Thelis ghamisi?

You're on!

θέλω να με σχίσεις

(I want you to tear me up)
pronounced: Thelo na me schisis

The brush—off

Αι γαμήσου

(Get fucked)
pronounced: Ai ghamisou

Hungarian

Hungarian is spoken in Hungary (also known locally as the Country of the Magyars) and surrounding states, and is related to Finnish. I could make a terrible pun about malnourishment at this point, but I fear this book may be taken off the shelves if I did.

Fancy a shag?

Van kedved dugni?

(Fancy a shag?)
pronounced: Von ked–ved doog(ə)nee?
(the 'oo' is short)

Akarsz szeretkezni?

(Fancy a shag?)
pronounced: Okars seret-keznee?

You're on!

Igen, szívesen

(Yes, please)
pronounced: Eegen, siveshen

The brush-off

Sajnálom, buzi vagyok/házas vagyok

(No, I'm gay/I'm married)
pronounced: Shainaləm, booze
wayok/hazash wayok
('ai' rhymes with 'by', 'a' is as in 'cat',
not 'way', 'oo' is short)

Icelandic

Nicknamed 'the Land of Fire and Ice', Iceland is a geologist's wet dream, and its people proudly boast of their nation as being the most expensive in the world. Due to volcanic activity, the island is steadily growing, and it is believed the people there are working on subtle world-domination schemes, waiting for the day when they have the largest country on Earth. Icelandic's closest living relative is Faroese, and it is thought to be the Scandinavian language closest to Old Norse.

Fancy a shag?

Viltu sofa hjá?

(Fancy a shag?)
pronounced: Viltø sova h–yau?
('ø' is like 'earl' but with lips slightly rounded)

You're on!

Já takk!

(Yes please!)
pronounced: Ya(r) tak!
(the 'r' is very faint and is closer to 'w' –
like Jonathan Ross's 'r's)

The brush-off

Farðu í rassgat!

(Fuck off!)
pronounced: Farthø ee rasskat!
('th' as in 'the', not 'thing', the last 'a'
is as in 'cat', but long)

Irish

Spoken in the Republic of Ireland, Northern Ireland, and Newfoundland, Canada. It is most similar to Scots Gaelic (although you can tell them apart in their writing, as the accents go different ways). Irish has also, to some extent, modernised its spelling to counter that oh-so-Gaelic spelling rule of 'why use three letters when you can use eight?' However they have not forgone the grammatical rule of 'why use five words when you can use fifteen?'

Fancy a shag?

An féidir liom deoch a cheannach duit?

(Can I buy you a drink? - very important in
Ireland, according to stereotype)
pronounced: Un fay-djur I-yum djuch
uh chyan-uch ditch?
('ch' like in 'loch', except for in 'ditch')

'bhfuil fonn marcaíochta ort ?

(Fancy a shag?)
pronounced: Will fon markiachta ort?
('ch' like in 'loch')

You're on!

Tá, ba bhreá liom, a stail mhór

(Yes, I'd love to, you sexy beast)
pronounced: Tah, ba vra lyome, uh stal wor

The brush-off

Níl, agus fág an áit sula gcuirfinn scairt ar na gardaí

(No, get away before I call the police)
pronounced: Neel, agus fag an atch sooluh
goorheen skart air na gardy

Italian

Italian is spoken in... you guessed it, Italy! It has also found its way into several other countries, which are too many to name. Italian is the language most closely resembling Latin in spelling, grammar, and pronunciation. This isn't surprising, considering the Romans were known for invading other countries and bringing Latin with them. However, since the Romans, Italy has found it challenging to hold onto its imperialistic image and success, and is now famed for its spaghetti, the Mafia, and its incredible ability to look like a boot. So you fancy yourself as the next Casanova? Here are some phrases to help you on your way...

Fancy a shag?

Ci facciamo una scopata?

(Shall we sleep out together?)
pronounced: Tchee fa'tchamo oona skopata?

scopiamo?

(Sleep with me?)
pronounced: Skop-yamo?

You're on!

Va bene, allora prendo il cappotto

(Yeah, ok then, I'll get my coat)
pronounced: Vah ('a' as in 'father') beynə, allora
(strong 'l') preyndle cappotto

The brush-off

Neanche se mi paghi

(Not even if you paid me)
pronounced: Neyanchey sey mee pagee

Te lo sogni, porco/maniaco

(Still dream about it/dream on, pig/maniac)
pronounced: Tey lo sonyee, porko/maneeako

Japanese

Japanese is spoken in Japan, as well as a number of other surrounding countries. Its writing system is based on the Chinese logograms (characters representing a word or morpheme), and it has a set of syllabic characters which are also based on the Chinese. However the two languages are not related. Japan is known for its earthquakes, gruesome movies, cute cartoons, electrical companies, martial arts, school girls, and raw fish.

Fancy a shag?

やらせて

(Fancy a shag? – male to female)
pronounced: Yarasete?

しようか？

(Shall we?)
pronounced: Shiyoka?

終電大丈夫？

(Don't you worry about the last train? –
male to female)
pronounced: Shuden daijobu?

うち来る？

(Will you come to my room?)
pronounced: Uchi kuru?

You're on!

うん

(No [I don't care about the last train,
I want to stay with you until morning],
or yes [informal slang])
pronounced: Un

The brush-off

やだ

(No [informal slang])
pronounced: Yada

もう帰る

(I have to go)
pronounced: Mou kaeru

ありえない！
(Impossible!)
pronounced: Arienai!

結婚してるんだ
(I'm married)
pronounced: Kekkon shiterunda

ゲイなんだ
(I'm gay)
pronounced: Gei nanda

Kipsigis

This is spoken mainly in the Rift Valley Province in Kenya, and is closely related to Nandi, Keiyo, South Tugen, and Cherangany. The Kipsigis people are from the Kenyan Kalenjin tribe, who make up about 12% of Kenya's population. The term Kalenjin comes from a Nandi expression meaning 'I say (to you)'.

Fancy a shag?

Imuche iruu ak anee?

(Will you sleep with me?)
pronounced: roughly as written

Aninyoon akumin

(Will you sleep with me? – slang)
pronounced: roughly as written

Nyoon asurin

(Will you sleep with me? – more coarse slang)
pronounced: roughly as written

You're on!

Eeh

(Yes)
pronounced: roughly as written

Kumon

(Yes – used more in the sex context)
pronounced: roughly as written

The brush-off

A shake of the head or slap in the face most likely...

Korean

Spoken in Korea! Both North and South, and parts of China. Korean is thought to be a language isolate (meaning it is not related to any other languages), although its writing system was originally based on Chinese characters. However now it mainly uses an alphabetical system, and also employs spaces between words, unlike Chinese and Japanese. North and South Korean have differences in pronunciation, spelling, grammar and vocabulary. These phrases are South Korean, so check a compass before going out on the pull!

Fancy a shag?

나랑 잘래?

(Fancy a shag?)
pronounced: Narang jal-lae?

You're on!

좋아

(Yes)
pronounced: Jo ah

The brush-off

꺼져!

(Piss off!)
pronounced: Ggu ju!
(the 'g' is in between 'c' and 'g' so its pronounced
softer than 'c' but stronger than 'g')

Latin

Although technically dead, Latin is still used in a whole variety of situations – religious, legal, as well as the good old Latin schoolroom. So, should you want to chat up a priest, lawyer, Latin teacher, student, or academic, (or in fact happen to invent a working time machine and travel back 2000 years, feeling randy) these are the phrases to use...

Fancy a shag?

Dorme mecum

(Sleep with me)
pronounced: Dormey meycum ('u' as in 'put')

You're on!

Apudne te vel me?

(Your place or mine?)
pronounced: Apudney tey wel mey?

The brush-off

Ut si!

(As if!)
pronounced: Ut see!
('ut' rhymes with 'put')

Futue te ipsum

(Go fuck yourself)
pronounced: Futoo-ey tey ipsum
('u' as in 'put')

Es scortum obscenus vilis

(You are a vile, perverted whore)
pronounced: Eys scortum obsenus
wilis ('u' as in 'put')

Pig Latin

This is a language game thought to have originated in German prisoner-of-war camps. These days it is usually employed by children in an effort to conceal conversations from adults. However, it is so simple that most people who used it in their youth will still understand it. These phrases could be used for ensnaring an unsuspecting youth (though not advised if you don't fancy spending some time behind bars) or charming your target by showing that you are in touch with your inner child.

Fancy a shag?

Ancyfay a-hay hagsay?

(Fancy a shag?)
pronounced: as written

You're on!

Esyay leasepay, ouyay inkykay atray

(Yes please you kinky rat)
pronounced: as written

The brush-off

Onay, odsay ffo-hay ouyay irtyday ervertpay

(No, sod off you dirty pervert)
pronounced: as written

Latvian

Latvian is part of the Eastern Baltic language group, and is spoken in Latvia in North East Europe. It is related to Lithuanian, however the two languages are not mutually intelligible. Explicit sex-language is not commonly used, so the phrases opposite use very subtle hints, referring to the Latvian summer solstice festival of Līgo, where it is believed that the ferns bloom on just that night each year. On this night the people dance, drink, and the young people go into the forest to 'search for fern flowers' (or rather, they go off for a quick bit of sex). Mind that while the phrase is likely to be understood, it is not applicable to all times of the year, and you may just attract a curious look (and perhaps a few horticultural enthusiasts).

Fancy a shag?

Eijam papardziedus meklēt

(Let's go search for fern flowers)
pronounced: Eh-yum papardziadus meklet
(last 'e' long, stress generally on the first syllable)

You're on!

Eijam!

(Let's go!)
pronounced: Eh-yum!

The brush-off

Pats meklē

(Go search yourself)
pronounced: Pats mek-le (last 'e' long)

Lithuanian

An Eastern Baltic language like Latvian, it is spoken in Lithuania, also a country in North East Europe. There are no other living Baltic languages beside Latvian and Lithuanian. Go to Lithuania, they have nice architecture and nice people.

Fancy a shag?

Norėtum pasidulkinti?

(Fancy a shag?)
pronounced: Nohreytuhm pahsihdoolkihntih?

You're on!

Taip, kodėl gi ne?

(Yes, why not?)
pronounced: Type, kohdeyl gih neh?

The brush-off

Dink iš čia, kol ne vėlu!

(Get away, while it's not too late! [a threat])
pronounced: Dink ihsh cheh, kohl nehveyloo!

Mandarin

Mandarin is a spoken dialect of Chinese, one of the main three along with Wu and Cantonese, and it is the official spoken language of the Republic of China. The Chinese writing system is made up of logograms, which represent morphemes (a meaningful unit of language), some of which are pictograms and some which are phonetic. It's too complicated to describe in a few sentences, and though similar, the written forms of the Chinese dialects are not identical. Both Mandarin and Cantonese are tonal languages, so a different tone given to a syllable can change the whole meaning of the word. The pronunciation guide here is rough, but hopefully you will be understood by a native speaker.

Fancy a shag?

和我做爱，好吗？
(Fancy a shag?)
pronounced: He wo zuo ai, hao ma?

You're on!

好的，在外面等我10分钟。
(Yes please, meet you outside in 10 minutes)
pronounced: Hao de, zai wai mian deng wo 10 fen zhong

The brush-off

不，走开，你这个性变态。
(No, go away you pervert)
pronounced: Bu, zou kai, ni zhe ge xing bian tai

Mauritian Creole

Mauritian Creole is a language based on French and spoken in Mauritius. A creole is formed when a pidgin language becomes a speaker's native language. As pidgins do not have sufficient grammar to function as primary languages, they evolve into creoles. Pidgins are formed when two languages meet, and neither group will learn the other's language. The pidgin becomes a mixture of the two, with one of the languages as its main base. These languages were developed in America, for example, by African slaves who were from different countries and spoke different languages, and needed to communicate with each other. Pidgin also evolved when Chinese traders came into contact with the British, but thought it beneath them to learn English and would not teach their language to the British. Pidgins are very basic, with the simplest grammatical structure and very small vocabularies.

Fancy a shag?

Tolé ène role are mwa?

(Fancy a shag?)
Pronounced: Tolay (like in 'today') an roll are mwa?

You're on!

Wouai!

(Yes!)
pronounced: Wey!

The brush—off

Non!

(No!)
pronounced: (as in French) No(n)!
(stop before you pronounce the
'n' so the 'o' is nasalized)

Norwegian

Norwegian is spoken in Norway, a country famous for its fjords, its parrots appearing in Monty Python sketches pining for said fjords, and its invasions of other countries back in pre-history. As a Scandinavian language, it is related to Swedish and Danish, and generally mutually intelligible with the two. Norwegian has two written forms, Bokmål and Nynorsk – Bokmål being the most common and most similar to Danish. Spoken dialects will differ again from the written forms.

Fancy a shag?

Hypp på et nyp?

(Fancy a shag?)
pronounced: Hip paw et nip (long 'y' in 'nyp')?

Lysten på et nummer?

(Do you want a quickie?)
pronounced: List–en paw et nommer?

Skal vi knulle?

(Shall we shag? – more crude)
pronounced: Skal (as you would pronounce the
Norwegian toast) vi (short 'i' as in 'Vicky') knullə?
('ull' as in 'pull', 'k' and 'n' are both pronounced)

You're on!

Hvorfor ikke?

(Why not?)
pronounced: Hvorfor ikə?
(the first 'o' rhymes with the first 'o' in 'Zorro')

Ja, takk – hos deg eller meg?

(Yes please – your place or mine?)
pronounced: Yah takk
(short 'a', hard 'k') – hus dye
('u' as in 'put') eller my?

The brush-off

Reis til helvete!

(Go to hell!)
pronounced: Race till hellvetey!
('ve' as in 'vet')

Kyss meg i raeva!

(Kiss my ass!)
pronounced: Kiss (although the 'i'
sounds more German) my ee reva!

Papiamentu

This is a creole language based mainly on Portuguese, and is spoken in Aruba, Curaçao and Bonaire. It was formed from a pidgin of Portuguese and Judeo-Portuguese spoken by Jews and their slaves, who had fled Dutch Brazil after it was taken over by the Portuguese.

Fancy a shag?

Bo ke chinga?

(Will you fuck with me?)
pronounced: Poh kə ching-ga?

You're on!

Si no... chingami duru!

(Yes... fuck me hard!)
pronounced: See naw... ching-gaamee dooroo!

The brush-off

No! Bai den konyo bo mama

(No! You motherfucker)
pronounced: Naw! Buy deen* kaw-yaw mo-mama
(*this vowel is short)

Patois/Jamaican Creole

This creole is English/African based and spoken in Jamaica. Although the creole is very similar to English, a non-Jamaican speaker would find it difficult to understand Patois unless it was slowed down, pronounced carefully, and most Jamaican slang left out – pronunciation and vocabulary are quite different from English dialects. The Jamaicans are famed for their rum and laid-back attitude to life (as demonstrated by Caribbean Rum and Lilt adverts) – don't worry if you don't get these phrases right the first time; just relax, man.

Fancy a shag?

Let ti go mek it run

(Can I have an orgasm – lit. 'let it go, make it run')
pronounced: as written, with Jamaican accent

You're on!

A–rite den, wa time, a whey?

(Ok then, what time and where?)
pronounced: as written, with Jamaican accent

The brush–off

Mi no kno bout dat

(I'm not sure about that)
pronounced: as written, with Jamaican accent

Polish

Polish is mainly spoken in Poland, and countries surrounding Poland. Polish belongs to a branch of the Western Slavic languages, and used to be pretty important as a language in Eastern Europe, before the spread and dominance of Russian. Due to Poland's recent welcome into the EU fold, the Poles are known for coming to our country and stealing our menial labour jobs traditionally reserved for students. Should you wish to catch a Pole more locally to practise your new-found linguistic skills on, they can usually be found queuing outside the temping agency at 5am, as they know they are guaranteed a job because no-one else will get up that early.

Fancy a shag?

Chcesz się ze mną przespać?

(Do you want to sleep with me?)
pronounced: Khtsesh shyeh zeh
mno(m)* pshespachy?
*the vowel here is nasal (said through the nose)

Chcesz się pieprzyć?

(Do you want to fuck?)
pronounced: Khtsesh shyeh pyepshechy?

Mogę ci wsadzić?

(Can I put it into you? –
only used by men, very vulgar)
pronounced: Mogeh chyi fsajyichy?

You're on!

Proste! Do mnie czy do ciebie?

(Sure! Your place or mine?)
pronounced: Prosteh! Do mnyeh chi do chyebyeh?

Jasne, mam całkiem fajną chatę!

(Ok, I have a pretty good flat!)
pronounced: Yasneh, mam tsawkyem
fayno(m)* khateh!
*the vowel here is nasal (said through the nose)

The brush-off

Nie, odpieprz się/spierdalaj!

(No, fuck off!)
pronounced: Nyeh, otpyepsh shyeh/spyerdalay!

Idź się jebać!

(Go fuck yourself!)
pronounced: Ijy shyeh yebachy!

N.B. Accent is always on the penultimate syllable,
here 'kh' represents 'ch' as in 'loch', and 'ch'
represents 'ch' as in 'church'. All 'o's are as in
'on', all 'a's are as in 'cat'.

Portuguese (Brazilian)

Portuguese is one of the major world languages and is spoken in Portugal, Brazil, Angola, Mozambique, and many other countries. Though these particular phrases are from Brazil, they would be understood by other Portuguese speakers. Brazil has brought us many vital commodities, such as Brazil nuts, the Brazilian (wax), and a fantastic national football team.

Fancy a shag?

Quer dormir comigo?

(Will you sleep with me?)
pronounced: Ker dohrmeer coomeegoo?

You're on!

Claro, espera só dez minutos que eu vou pegar o meu casaco

(Yes please, wait ten minutes and I'll get my coat)
pronounced: Klaroo, espera so des meenootoos ke ew vow piagar u meoo cazacoo

The brush-off

Cai fora!

(Piss off!)
pronounced: Kaee fora!

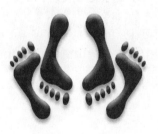

Romanian

Romanian is classed as a Romance language and is spoken mainly in Romania, Moldova, and Vojvodina in Serbia, and to a lesser extent in other surrounding countries. Romania notoriously houses the dreaded Count Dracula, so although these phrases are recommended if wanting to score with a Romanian, it may be advisable to take with you some extra garlic and a crucifix for protection, and ban any 'kinky' biting as a primary ground-rule.

Fancy a shag?

Vrei să te fuţi?

(Fancy a fuck?)
pronounced: Vrey sah teh foots'?
('r' is rolled, 'oo' as in 'boot', not 'foot')

You're on!

Da. Ştiu un loc grozav unde închiriază cu ora

(Yes. I know a great place where
they rent by the hour)
pronounced: Daa. Shtywu oon lawk grawzaav
oondeh ahnkeereeyazah koo awraa

The brush-off

Nu, du-te dracu(lui)

(No, go to hell)
pronounced: Noo, dooteh dhrawkoo(luy)!
('oo' is short, the 'lui')

Romany

This is the language of the Roma people, often called 'Gypsies', who are nomadic and originated between North West India and Iran. Now they live all over the world, primarily in Europe. Their language is related to languages of northern India, especially Punjabi, and loan words mark its peoples' migration westward. Dialects of Romany vary according to where they are spoken, for example Balkan Romany, Welsh Romany, Finnish Romany, etc. These phrases are from the Lovara dialect spoken in Romania, Hungary, Austria, and other East European countries.

Fancy a shag?

Kama dav bule tumende?

(Do you want to have sex with me?)
pronounced: Kama dav boolei toomeindei?

Kama buï–buï?

(Fancy a shag?)
pronounced: Kama booee– booee?

You're on!

Aj, avral ka maladivav tumende an deš xurdi

(Yes please, I'll meet you outside in 10 minutes)
pronounced: Aye, avral ka maladivav toomeindei an deish joordee

The brush-off

Ni, ha dža, lubikano dilo!

(No, come on get going, perverted madman!)
pronounced: Nee ha dja, loobikanow deelo!

Naš mora, gadžo!

(Get away, non-gypsy man/young man!)
pronounced: Nash maura, gadjo!

Buhlivav, chavo!

(Get stuffed, young man! – lit. get fat)
pronounced: Boohlivav tchavo!

Russian

Russian is a Slavic language written with the Cyrillic alphabet, and spoken in Russia and countries that used to be in the Soviet Union. The Russians are a friendly bunch, even if they don't like Chechnya. Their country is vast and cold (though not in the summer, although it is vast all year round) and has produced some very famous Communists. So order a double shot of vodka (not Smirnoff, get yourself some real vodka), put on your stupid furry hat, and flash your winning Rasputin smile...

Fancy a shag?

Хочешь трахнуться?

(Fancy a shag?)
pronounced: Hochesh trahnutsia?

Хочешь поебаться?

(Fancy a shag?)
pronounced: Hochesh poebatsia?

You're on!

Конечно, через пять минут в туалете

(Sure, 5 minutes in the toilet)
pronounced: Konechno, cherz p–yat minut v tualete

The brush-off

Нет, иди трахни сам себя, сука!

(No, how about you go shag yourself, you cunt!)
pronounced: Net, idi trajni sam sebia, suka!

Нет, отъябись, пизда!

(No, fuck off, bastard!)
pronounced: Net, otyabis, pizda!

Serbian

Serbian is spoken in the state of Serbia and Montenegro, and is mutually intelligible with Bosnian and Croatian. 'Serbia' is an anagram of 'rabies', and this should be borne in mind when you think that Serbia is the home of Kosovo, and dearest Slobodan Milosovic, who died in custody whilst being tried for crimes against humanity. However the Serbians are no doubt a friendly bunch (and if the only Serbian you can think of is Liljana Bishop from *Neighbours* then you need to get some culture in you) and chatting them up should be no bother, honest!

Fancy a shag?

Hoćeš da se kresnemo?

(Fancy a shag?)
pronounced: Hochesh da se kresnemo?

You're on!

Ej, može, vidimo se napolju za desetak minuta

(Yes please, see you outside in ten minutes)
pronounced: Ey, mozyey ('zy' like in the middle of 'vision'), videemo se napol-you za desetak minoota

The brush-off

Ma, odjebi, perverznjačino

(No, get lost, pervert)
pronounced: Ma, odyebee, perverzn-yacheeno

Sign language (British)

Of course, there is a proportion of the population who won't be able to understand your (very fair) request no matter how well you pronounce it. These signs are pretty universal, and even someone who doesn't know British Sign Language should be able to get the gist of what you're saying. It helps to mouth the words as you do the actions – so the phrase (in words) would go something like 'you, me, together, shag'.

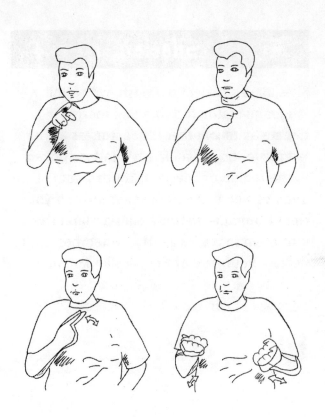

Silesian

Silesian is a dialect of Polish, with similar language status to Scots (i.e. there is debate as to whether it qualifies as a true language, or just a dialect), and is spoken in the region of Silesia in South West Poland and the North East Czech Republic. If you were hoping to flatter a Silesian (and thus lure them into your bed) it would be best to declare your love of the Silesian *language*.

Fancy a shag?

Mogymy sie onacyć?

(Fancy a shag?)
pronounced: Mogimee shiu onuhsich?

You're on!

'ja, pudymy za winkel i pokoża ci jak to je

(Yes please, meet you outside in ten minutes)
pronounced: Ya pudoomoo zə
vinkəl ə pokoza shak too
('u' here is as in 'put')

The brush-off

Njy, śmigoj stond jerunie jedyn

(No, get lost, pervert)

pronounced: Nee, shmeego stont yeroon yaydən

Slovenian

Slovenian is a Slavic language spoken in Slovenia. Slovenia is one of our newest EU member states, and we love it dearly. These phrases are examples of slang, as would be spoken in Slovenia's capital, Ljubljana...

Fancy a shag?

A' s' za fuk?

(Fancy a shag?)
pronounced: As za fook?

A' b' spala z mano?

(Will you sleep with me?)
pronounced: Ab spala zmano?

You're on!

Ja, se vid'va zun(i) čez deset minut

(Yes, meet you outside in 10 minutes)
pronounced: Yah, sə veedva zoon(y)
cheyz deset meenoot

The brush-off

Ne, "spizdi", perverznež!

(No, piss off you pervert!)
pronounced: Ne, speezdy perverznesh!

Somali

Somali is spoken in Somalia and Somaliland (East coast of Africa), as well as Djibouti, Ethiopia and Kenya. Somalia has a turbulent history of civil war, and while you won't necessarily be pinned down by machine-gun fire on a regular basis should you choose to visit, that's not to say you won't get shot... But hey, you could say that about Nottingham!

Fancy a shag?

Ma dooneysaa inaan isu galmoonno?

(Do you want to have sex with me?)
pronounced: Ma do-ney-saa e-naan
esu gal-mo-no?

You're on!

Haa waan doonayaa!

(Yes I'd love to!)
pronounced: Haa waan do-na-yaa!

The brush-off

Maya, igatag qurunyahow!

(No, get away from me you freak!)
pronounced: Ma-ya ega-tag qu-run-ya-how!

Spanish

Spanish is one of the four most spoken languages in the world, so these phrases will prove invaluable. You will find Spanish spoken as a national language in Spain, as well as in some South American countries, and there are immigrant speakers all over the world. The dialects across these countries will vary – these phrases are Spanish Spanish, best used for pulling in Madrid. Go on – take the bull by the horns and snag a matador (*groan* these are getting worse... but I will keep trying).

Fancy a shag?

¿Te querès acostar conmigo?

(Will you sleep with me?)
pronounced: Tay kerres ah-coast-ar con-me-go?

¿Qué te apetece echar un polvo?

(Fancy a shag?)
pronounced: Kay tay ah-pet-eh-thay
eh-char oon paul-vo?

Quiero follar

(I'd like to shag you)
pronounced: Kee-a-ro foh-yar

You're on!

Si, tengo ganas

(Yes, I want)
pronounced: See, ten-go gah-nahs

Si, de Puta Madre!

(Yes, fucking yes! (lit. Mother of Bitches))
pronounced: See, deh poo-tah mah-dray!

The brush-off

No tengo ganas

(No I don't want)
pronounced: No ten-go gah-nahs

No, que te jodes

(No, get fucked)
pronounced: No, key tey hodes

Swahili

This is a Bantu language spoken in many countries across East Africa from Somali to Mozambique. The name 'Swahili' comes from an Arabic word meaning 'coastal dwellers', and so, strangely, the people who speak it live in coastal regions.

Fancy a shag?

Unaweza kufanya ngono nami?

(Will you sleep with me?)
pronounced: as written

Kamu tudoro pamoja/kamu nikudare?

(Fancy a shag?)
pronounced: as written

You're on!

Ndiyo/eeh/we kamu/nidare

(Yes)
pronounced: as written

The brush-off

Hapana!

(No!)
pronounced: as written

Huyu ni mke (mume) wangu

(Meet my wife (husband))
pronounced: as written

Swedish

Swedish is spoken in Sweden and in parts of Finland, and is mutually intelligible with Danish and Norwegian. The population of Sweden is half that of London, and this is believable as you fly over the country and see just trees, lakes, trees, lakes, trees, lakes, trees, road, trees, lakes, trees, lakes, oh, and a house! If you say the word 'Swedish' what often tends to follow is 'porn star', and an image of Sweden is simply filled with beautiful people (a pleasing myth, unfortunately). With these thoughts close to your heart, and these words safe in your pocket, go out there and embrace some stereotypes! (Quite literally!)

Fancy a shag?

Vill du knulla?

(Fancy a shag?)
pronounced: Veel doo knoola?
(the 'ee' is short)

You're on!

O ja, din sexiga best

(Oh yes, you sexy beast)
pronounced: Oh yah, deen sexeega best

The brush-off

Nej, din fitta/snuskhummer!

(No, you cunt/dirty old man! (lit. dirty lobster))
pronounced: Ney, deen fyitta/snooks-hoomer!
(the 'y' in 'fyitta' is very soft, almost
not pronounced, so that the 'i' has a
different sound to English 'i')

Thai

...spoken in Thailand, is a tonal language similar, in that respect, to Chinese. Thailand is famous for its beaches, brothels, and stunning lady-boys - watch out for these if you're hoping for a girl without a penis. The country is also a favourite with students seeking to 'find themselves', and drug smugglers. A great time to be had by all! You *know* these phrases are going to be helpful...

Fancy a shag?

จะไปต่อที่ไหน

(Fancy a shag?)

pronounced: Cha pai taw tee nai?

You're on!

บ้านคุณ บ้านผม หรือโรงแรม

(Your place, or mine, or a hotel?)

pronounced: Baan Khun baan
phom reu rong-raem?

The brush–off

ไม่ว่าง--
(I'm not available)
pronounced: Mai waang

ไว้วันหลัง
(Maybe later)
pronounced: Wai wan lang

Turkish

Turkish is spoken mainly in Turkey and Cyprus, and is an immigrant language in many European countries, notably Germany. Historically, the Turks and the Greeks haven't got on, and Turkey (not to be confused with Christmas poultry) used to be in possession of the vast Ottoman Empire, conquering much of the Middle East and Mediterranean. The Turkish are those wonderful people who brought us belly dancing, kebabs, Turkish baths, and soap-flavoured sweets. Mmmm, sexy.

Fancy a shag?

Çılgın sevişme?

(Fancy a shag?)
pronounced: Chølgøn sayveshmeh?
('ch' as in 'loch', 'ø' as in 'earl',
but with rounded lips)

Sikişmek ister misin?

(Would you like to fuck?)
pronounced: Seekeeshmaik eestair meeseen?

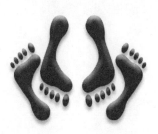

You're on!

Ah evet, seni seksi şempanze

(Ah yes please, you sexy beast (chimpanzee))
pronounced: Ahh evet seenee sexsi shempanzay

The brush-off

Siktir git

(Go fuck off!)
pronounced: Seekteer geet!

Ukranian

Spoken in the Ukraine and in other neighbouring Slavic nations. Ukraine is another nation brought to Western European attention by its Eurovision victory, although it is a country perhaps better known in connection with the former Soviet Union. Don't confuse its people with Russians, they won't like it and it won't get you laid.

Fancy a shag?

Ну що, п┐ демо до л┐ жечка?
(Will you sleep with me?)
pronounced: Nu sho, pidemo do lizhechka?

You're on!

Добре, т┐ льки зачекай хвилиночку!
(Yes please, meet you outside in 10 minutes!)
pronounced: Dobre, til'ki zachekaj hvylynochku!

The brush-off

Геть в┐ д мене, покидьок!
(No sod off you pervert!)
pronounced: Get' vid mene, pokidyok!

Welsh

There are simply not enough sheep-shagging jokes in the world to use when mentioning the Welsh and sex. The Welsh language is of the Brythonic P-Celtic branch along with Cornish and Breton, and since the popularity of minority language preservation and revival, is a great source of national pride. However if a group of Welsh speakers hears a remotely English accent in its midst, it is 98% likely to hold the rest of the conversation entirely in Welsh. Therefore, if you happen to have an English accent, these phrases will put you in good stead. However, if you find them difficult to master, another option is to stand in a field and bleat until someone comes by...

Fancy a shag?

Beth am y gwely?

(What about going to bed?)
pronounced: Beth am ə gwellooh?

T'isio rhyw?

(Do you want sex?)
pronounced: Too-shoh roouh?

You're on!

Iawn, bishyn

(Ok, gorgeous)
pronounced: Yaun, bish-oohn

The brush-off

Dos i ganu

(Go and sing)
pronounced: Doss ee gan(uh)

Dos i falu awyr

(Go and smash the sky)
pronounced: Doss ee valooh awuhr

Yiddish

'Yiddish' is the Yiddish word for 'Jewish', and the language itself is very similar to German. It is now spoken by Jewish communities all around the world, especially in the United States. Yiddish is usually written using the Hebrew writing system, but can also be written using the Roman alphabet. If the only Jewish stereotypes you can think of are Shylock from Shakespeare's *Merchant of Venice*, Topol in *Fiddler on the Roof*, or Barbara Streisand in *Yentl*, then you need to get out more...

Fancy a shag?

Vilst du yentzen?

(Fancy a shag?)
pronounced: Vilst doo yentzen?

Lomir shtupen/lomir zetzen

(Let's shag)
pronounced: Lomeer shtoopen/lomeer zetzen
('oo' as in 'put')

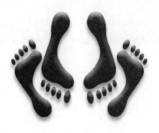

You're on!

Biteh!

(Please!)
pronounced: Bitteh!

Dos gefelt mir

(This pleases me)
pronounced: Dos gəfelt meer

Es ken gemolt zein

(It is conceivable/It is imaginable)
pronounced: Ess ken gəmolt zine

The brush-off

Gei tren zich!

(Go screw yourself!)
pronounced: Gay tren zich!

Kush mir in tuches!

(Kiss my ass!)
pronounced: Koosh meer in toochəss!
('oo' as in 'put' or 'book')

Bareh nisht!

(Don't fuck with me!)
pronounced: Bareh nisht!
N.B. 'ch' is as in Scottish 'loch'

Acknowledgements

To Stu, Kyle, and Iain

Without the help of many, many people, this book would never have found its way to completion. I would like to give my heart-felt thanks to (in no particular order):

Stu Dunmore, Simon Ager, Steve Hewitt, Alice Lo, Nigel Hathaway, Natalie Farmer, Irem Sereofogl, Judith Schwegler, Sacha Zatcheshigriva, Sophia Friedrich, Christian Hemfort, Florian Halbritter, Dr. Mads Gabrielsen, Ramez Bishawi, Katie Beedham, Roland Schaap, Iwan Lecorre, Nanna Jonsson, Moha Aden, Mirka Hlavacova, Molly Park, Helge K. Fauskanger, Leelou Cziernak, Antoni Brosa, Kairi Ostrat, Mai, Gennadiy Guskov, Patrick Langat, Mladen Tomic, Wikipedia, Lyle Milne, Michele Zampollo, Rainer Yalung, the Tolkien language guild Mellonath Daeron, Eugene Robertus, Johan Petur Dam, Nadine van den Abbeele, Winsome Lennon, Jaka Jakopic, Leandros Markid, Graeme McKinnon, Lawrence Edmonds, Csaba Gosswein, Fabien Fouquet, Oliver Hathaway, Jakob Schleicher, Lien Van Malderen, Zarya Rathe, Rags Seatter, Carlos Afonso, The Grey Company (www.grey-company.org), Shane Gilchrist Ó hEorpa.